REX

Book #1 in the TIME SOLDIERS® Series

Created and Photographed by Robert Gould
Digitally Illustrated by Eugene Epstein
Written by Robert Gould and Kathleen Duey

The woods smelled like rain. Squirrels and rabbits scattered, startled by the passing bikes.

"I can't wait!" Mikey yelled to his big brother. Rob grinned. He was excited too. In three days, they were going camping and exploring with their best friends. They'd saved all summer for camouflage fatigues and packs...even rafts and slingshots.

Suddenly, Mikey braked, his bike skidding sideways. Rob swerved to miss him, trying to focus on the strange swirling light. This couldn't be real. A *dinosaur?* Rob flinched as it lifted its head to look at them.

"Run!" Rob screamed, stumbling backward. They raced for home.

Minutes later, Rob tried to describe the weird
swirling trees and the dinosaur. Mom and Dad
enjoyed the story...but they didn't believe it.

He finally gave up. "We're going hiking." Rob said. "All six of us." Mikey nodded.
"OK, boys," Mom said. "Be home for lunch."

"Jon," Rob whispered into the phone. "Call Mariah. She can call Adam and Bernardo. Meet us at the clubhouse and — "

"What happened?" Jon interrupted.

"Just bring the gear and wear your camouflage," Rob told him. "And hurry."

Rob hung up, giving Mikey the thumbs-up sign. They changed, then checked their equipment. Mikey got out their slingshots. "We might need these," he said.

Rob opened his bottom drawer and took out the old video camera Dad had given him. If nothing he said could convince his parents, getting the dinosaur on *videotape* certainly would.

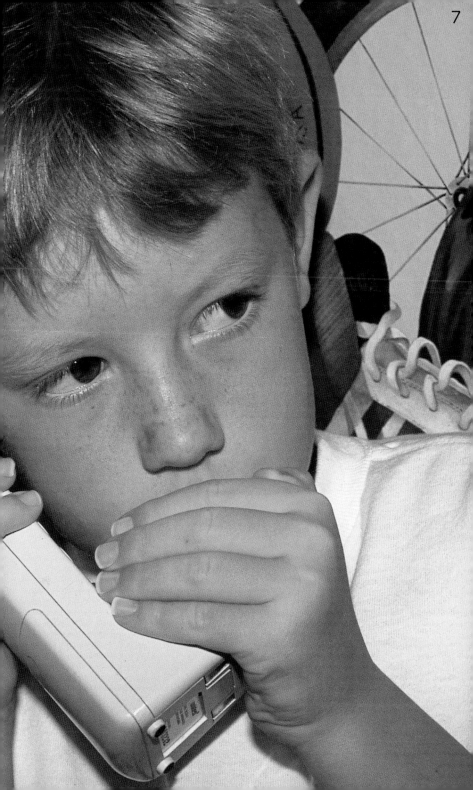

Half an hour later, the six friends stood staring
at the swirling tunnel...and two dinosaurs.
"Apatosaurus," Mariah murmured.
"Can we go in there?" Jon whispered.

"We could explore it," Rob said. Adam nodded.
Mikey looked at Rob. "Let's do it!"
Rob and Jon led them forward.
Bernardo hesitated, then followed.

Rob took a deep breath. The air was sweet with the smell of fresh lake water. The forest was so lush, so incredibly clean.

"Apatosaurus," Mariah repeated quietly. "They weighed 30 tons! Scientists argue about whether or not they lived in water."

"They seem to like wading," Rob said. His voice sounded strangely out of place here. It was so quiet he could hear the sound of his own heartbeat.

A rustling of wings overhead made them all whirl around.

"What *is* that?" Bernardo asked.

Rob raised the video camera and framed the flying reptile, zooming in to get a good look. It was huge. He glanced at Bernardo. "Those wings must be 20 feet across."

"Quetzalcoatlus," Mariah told them.

"But that doesn't make any sense because — "

"Is it dangerous?" Rob asked.

The uncertain look on Mariah's face told him all he needed to know. "Head for the trees!" he shouted, pushing Mikey ahead of him as they all began to run.

Rob counted helmets. Six. Everyone was safe...so far. The ground trembled, startling him. He turned, raising the video cam.

"Tyrannosaurus Rex," Mariah whispered. "Don't move."

Through the viewfinder, Rob focused on a leg as big as a tree trunk. His heart pounded...

10:47(X250%)
● REC

It moved toward them. Adam flinched. "Run!"
Rob grabbed his arm. "No! Don't!!"

"Motion will attract it," Mariah said.

Bernardo was trembling. Jon put a reassuring arm around him. "It'll be OK," he said.

Adam closed his eyes. Mikey stood as still as a rock, his fists tightly clenched.

The ground shuddered beneath the Tyrannosaur's massive weight as it moved through the brush. Then, abruptly, the dinosaur stopped. Rob heard branches breaking...then a dull tearing sound.

"It's feeding," Mariah whispered. "Its kill must be on the other side of those bushes."

Rob zoomed in for a better look.

"We can't stay this close," Adam said in a shaky voice, stepping back.

Rob turned to grab him, but Adam was already moving away. Bernardo jumped up to follow.

Then, in stunned silence, Rob watched as the T-Rex slowly lifted its huge head...

"Run!" Jon shouted, shoving at Rob.

Mariah yelled something, but her voice was lost in the thunder of the Tyrannosaur's roar...a sound that made Rob's teeth vibrate. Running was useless. "Climb!" he shouted. "Hide in the trees!"

Mikey found a low branch and started climbing.

10:55(X100%)
● REC

Rob followed him, clutching the video cam tightly. Once he and his brother were on a sturdy limb, he glanced back. Jon and Adam were in a tree across the clearing. Mariah and Bernardo were closer. They looked terrified.

The T-Rex was staring right at them.

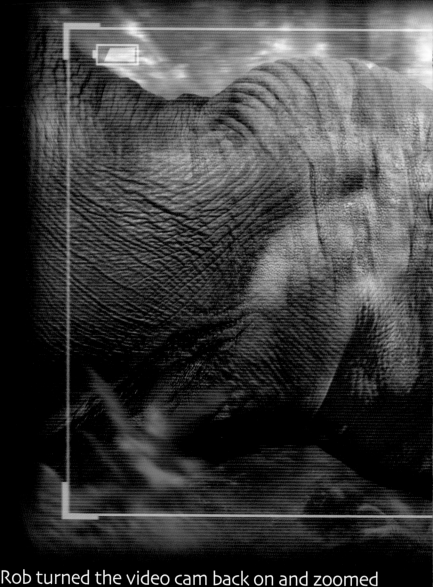

Rob turned the video cam back on and zoomed in. He could see the giant nostrils flare with each breath. Beyond the T-Rex, he saw the kill, a small Triceratops. A darting motion caught Rob's eye. He lowered the camera. Two smaller dinosaurs were running through the forest, toward T-Rex's unguarded supper.

10:58(X10%)
●REC

"Velociraptors..." Mariah shuddered.
"They're fast," Rob whispered as he
pointed. Mikey nodded.
One of the scavengers was already tearing off
a big chunk of meat...with needle-sharp teeth.
As it did, another horrendous roar exploded
into the air. T-Rex had seen the raptors.

One of them looked up defiantly. The T-Rex attacked, its jaws closing around the raptor's neck. There was a sickening crunch...then an eerie silence.

The Tyrannosaur lifted its head, looking for
the other raptor. Rob turned off the camera
and scanned the bushes. Where *was* it?

"Rob, watch out!" In the silence, Jon's voice was startling.

"Shhh!" Rob hissed at him.

Then Mikey pointed downward, his face pale. Rob twisted around.

The second Velociraptor scratched wildly at the tree trunk, leaping up, snapping at his foot.

Rob jerked his leg upward, nearly losing his balance. The raptor jumped again...

A volley of sharp rocks spattered the tree trunk and the raptor's hide. Angered, it turned to face Mariah and Bernardo standing at the foot of their tree.

It took a leap toward them, then stopped as they reloaded and fired again. Rob heard the rocks hit hard. Shrieking, the raptor spun, then leapt away, disappearing into the trees.

That was too close, Rob thought to himself.
He lifted the video cam, zooming in to get a
final shot of the raptor as it ran away.

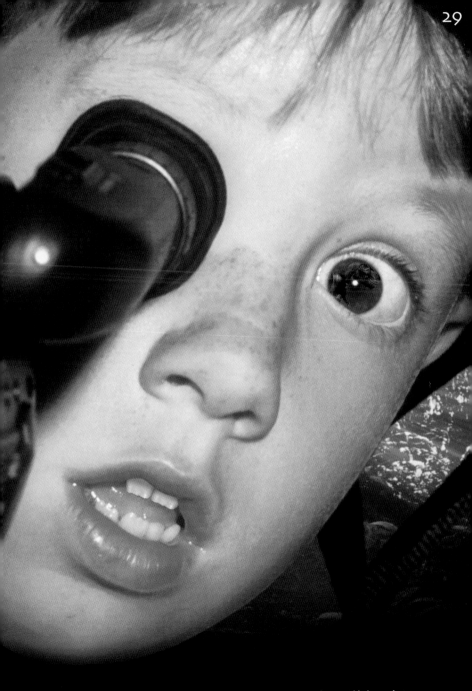

Then he swung back around, still looking
through the camera and ...

Rob caught his breath.

"Oh no..." Mikey turned. "It sees us."

11.11(X400%)

● REC

The Tyrannosaurus wasn't as close a
through the zoom lens, but it was n
close for comfort, and it was starinç
now. There was only one thing they

"Run for the river!" Rob shouted, scrambling downward. He made sure Mikey was running the right direction, then looked across the clearing. He could see the T-Rex moving through the trees.

Mariah was in the lead. Bernardo had slowed so Mikey could catch up. Jon was running hard, dodging trees and bushes. Rob and Adam followed close behind.

Mikey stumbled. Rob glanced back. The T-Rex was getting closer. Suddenly, Jon stopped and loaded a stone into his slingshot

Rob held his breath as his best friend took careful aim, drew back, then released...

ZZZzzzzzzaaap! The stone struck hard, right between the Tyrannosaur's eyes. Startled, roaring in fury, the dinosaur charged, shaking its massive head.

Jon bolted, leaping fallen logs and diving behind a clump of bushes.

Confused by the mysterious pain, the T-Rex smashed into a huge tree and fell sideways. The ground shook violently.

"Can you see the river?" Jon shouted.

"This way!" Rob yelled.

At the top of the ridge, Rob saw the white foam of rushing water below. Jon jumped, skidding down the muddy bluff. Rob followed. Within seconds, everyone was sliding...

Jon was leaning, guiding his slide like a muddy snowboarder. Rob imitated him...and yelled at Mikey to use his balance. The wild slide was turning into fun. Rob glanced back at the bluff. There was no sign of the Tyrannosaurus.

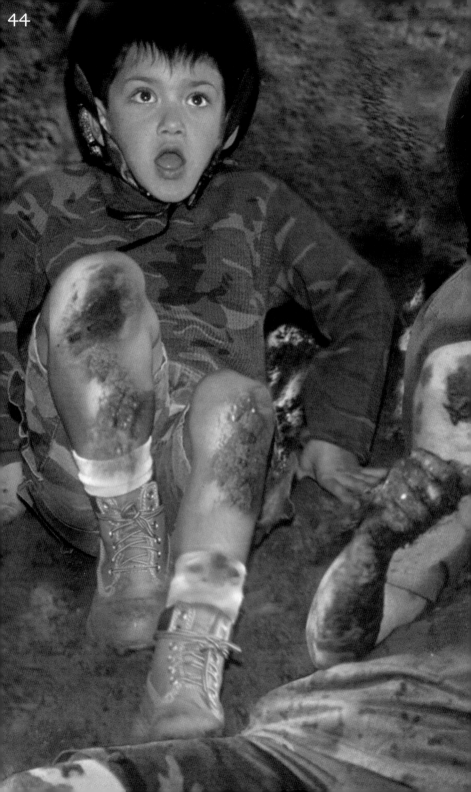

"We made it!" Jon shouted as the slope leveled out beside the river. Everyone cheered.

"Oh no," Bernardo said.

Rob looked up, then quickly scrambled to his feet.

Staring hungrily at them was the biggest lizard he had ever seen...

"Inflate the rafts!" Rob yelled, searching for a rock. "Hurry!" Seconds later, he heard air rushing into the valves. Focusing on the monster-sized lizard, he set his sight on its face, then changed his mind. There were no trees here to stop an enraged attack.

He shifted his aim to the beard-like pouch under its jaw. Rob exhaled, then released and reloaded in one smooth motion. The lizard leapt back, startled by the sudden pain. Rob shot a second time...and once more the lizard moved backward

"Get in!" Mariah was
yelling."

"Come on!" Mikey
shouted.

Rob backed up, watching
the lizard. It flicked its
tongue and turned away.
Rob ran down the bank
and jumped into the
second raft.

Jon, Adam, and Bernardo
were already in the
current, heading down-
stream. The water was
cold and swift. Rob
paddled quickly, trying
to catch up.

"We made it!" Mariah
shouted over the roaring
water.

Then she screamed...

Rob barely saw the giant rock through the whitewater mist. He dug his paddle in hard, steering the raft to the left. Mariah back paddled. They held their breath as the raft cleared the boulder by mere inches.

The two rafts shot downstream side by side.

"This is so cool," Jon grinned. "It's like we've been transported millions of years back in time."

"I just wish this place made sense," Mariah said as they entered quieter waters.

"We must have come through some sort of time portal," Rob said.

"Has to be," Jon agreed. "We're in prehistoric times."

Mariah frowned. "But some of these animals lived millions of years apart. I don't get it."

"Look," Adam pointed. "Triceratops."

"They belong here," Mariah said. "But the Apotasaurus doesn't and — "

"They look almost tame,"
Adam interrupted.

"They're grazers," Mariah said as the raft rounded a bend in the river, "not predators."

Mikey scooped up some clear water to drink. It was sweet and cold.

Bernardo pointed. "Apatosaurus?"

"Yeah," Mariah said. "More grazers...but from 77 million years *before* T-Rex."

3:54(X150%)
● REC

Rob turned the video cam back on. He knew everyone would be amazed by these tapes when they got home. *If* they ever did.

"Maybe we should go back toward the portal..." Rob began, and then stopped. The others shook their heads. No one was ready to go near the Tyrannosaurus yet.

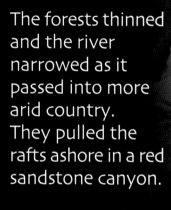

The forests thinned and the river narrowed as it passed into more arid country. They pulled the rafts ashore in a red sandstone canyon.

"No T-Rex here," Rob said. "No trees."

Mariah shrugged. "No one really knows where they lived."

"We'll tell 'em," Mikey joked. "Forests."

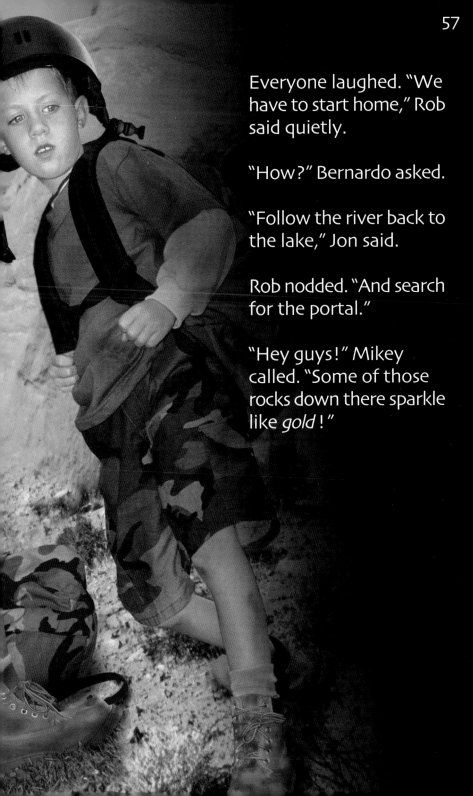

Everyone laughed. "We have to start home," Rob said quietly.

"How?" Bernardo asked.

"Follow the river back to the lake," Jon said.

Rob nodded. "And search for the portal."

"Hey guys!" Mikey called. "Some of those rocks down there sparkle like *gold*!"

"Look!" Adam yelled.
"There's a passageway!"

"I'm hungry," Bernardo
said quietly. No one
answered and he sighed.
"I want to go home."

"We all do," Adam said.
He led the way. It was
strange and beautiful
at the same time.

As Mikey walked, he
kept stopping to pick up
rocks, putting them into
his pockets.

Rob walked slowly,
thinking. What were they
going to do if they
couldn't find the portal?

The Quetzalcoatlus they had seen at the waterfall was circling above them. "It's just curious," Mikey said.

Mariah nodded. "Like the Triceratops and the Apatosaurus. They've never seen anything like us before."

The sun was hot and Rob
was getting tired, when a
sparkle in the rock made
him blink. He climbed
down and picked up a
glittering stone.

"It's gold." he whispered.
He opened his hand to
show Jon the shiny,
yellow metallic rock.

"Gold!" Jon shouted.
Everyone gathered to see.

"Look!" Bernardo said.
"Here's another piece!"

Mikey grinned. "Are we
going to be rich?"

"If I were rich, I'd buy
the skateboard store,"
Rob said.

Jon grinned. "I'd buy a
dirt bike and a go-cart!!"

Mariah laughed. "We could
give money away to kids
who don't have any!"

They spread out, searching the rocks for more nuggets.

"We have to keep going," Rob reminded them.

Mikey frowned. "I bet we could find a lot more gold if we could just stay a little longer..."

"Here," Rob said, handing Mikey the video cam. "Get a shot of me with this!"

Mikey was careful to hold the camera steady as he taped Rob with the gold against the amazing blue of the prehistoric sky.

4:50(X0X)
● REC

"We better get going," Jon said.

Rob sighed. "Let's go guys." Adam looked up from the gravel he was sifting. Bernardo stood, dusting off his shorts. Mariah squinted into the sun as they started off.

Rob kept the camera on. The scenery changed as they walked, and the river widened again.

"What's that sound?" Bernardo asked.

Rob listened. He shook his head. "A waterfall? The *lake* had a waterfall."

Mikey found a way down the steep ridge...
a great shortcut through the house-sized
boulders.

Everyone followed.

The waterfall was magnificent, but there was no river and no lake. The water bubbled up from underground springs, and then ran over the cliffs. Below, it roared into a crevasse that must have led to underground caverns and tunnels because the water simply disappeared.

5:17(×10%)
● REC

Rob videotaped a huge flower Mariah and Mikey found. She was smiling. "I noticed one of these just inside the portal, when we first came through..."

"I hope we can find it," Rob said wistfully.

"Hey, you guys!" Jon shouted.

Rob stared, astonished. Jon was walking on *nothing*...

"It feels weird, Rob," he laughed. "Try it!"

Rob went next, making sure it wasn't dangerous. It was like wading through an anti-gravity puddle.

"Where's Adam?" Jon asked suddenly. Everyone stopped joking and turned to look around.

"I don't believe it," Bernardo said, pointing. "Look!"

"A Centrosaurus!" Mariah gasped. "A *baby* one!!"

"Is Adam doing what I think he's doing?" Mikey asked. "Hey, there's a baby longneck too!"

Adam let the Centrosaurus sniff his hand. Then he climbed onto its back.

Everyone watched as Adam and the little
dinosaur played, tearing back and forth

Mikey tossed his pack
to Rob, then ran toward
the baby Apatosaurus.

Its mother looked at him closely.
The baby was curious and friendly.

Mikey patted the little dinosaur. It lowered its head and stared into Mikey's eyes. A moment later, he straddled its long neck. When it raised its head, he slid down onto its back.

It didn't notice his weight and followed its mother up the hill. Mikey rocked with the dinosaur's gait; its baggy skin felt cool against his legs.

On the ridge top, he looked down at a wide lake. In the dusk, he saw a waterfall at the far end. A towering forest grew along the shoreline.

"Rob!" he shouted. "There's the lake!" He jumped down and ran toward his friends.

"Can anyone see the portal?" Rob asked as they headed downhill.

"Not yet," Mariah answered. "But it has to be — "

"There!" Jon said. "I think…"

"I see it, too," Mikey said joyfully.

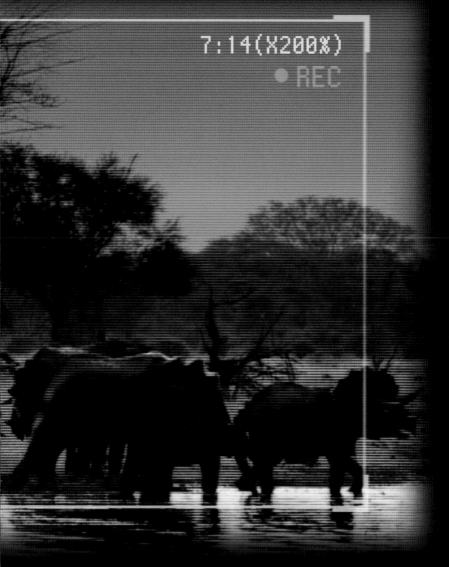

Rob raised the video cam and got a shot of the sunset-colored sparkle in the forest and the watering hole full of dinosaurs. The battery was almost dead. He zoomed in on the trees as the low battery warning sounded. A quick movement startled him...

The strange image in the viewfinder made Rob stumble backward. He lowered the camera and peered at the edge of the forest. But it was gone now.

"Rob? Are you all right?" Jon asked.

"Yeah..." he answered. "Hurry up you guys, it's getting dark."

They took off their packs and threw them in first. It seemed safe. Rob clutched the video cam close to his chest and walked forward...into the portal. He felt a tingling prickle on his skin.

Coming out of the portal, he saw the woods, *their* woods, in the morning sunlight.

Everything was calm and familiar.
It still smelled like rain.

"How can it *still* be morning?" Mikey asked.

No one answered.

"Let's get back to the clubhouse," Rob said. "We have to figure this out."

Jon nodded without saying anything.

They started off. Mariah glanced back. She blinked, startled.

"Wait you guys! Look, it's, it's…"

"Look at what?" Adam asked.
    Mariah blinked, then rubbed her eyes.
    Rob frowned. "There's nothing there."
    "Let's go," Mikey said.

Adam shrugged his pack higher on his shoulders. "Come on, Mariah. You're just tired."

She glanced back once more, then followed the boys up the path.

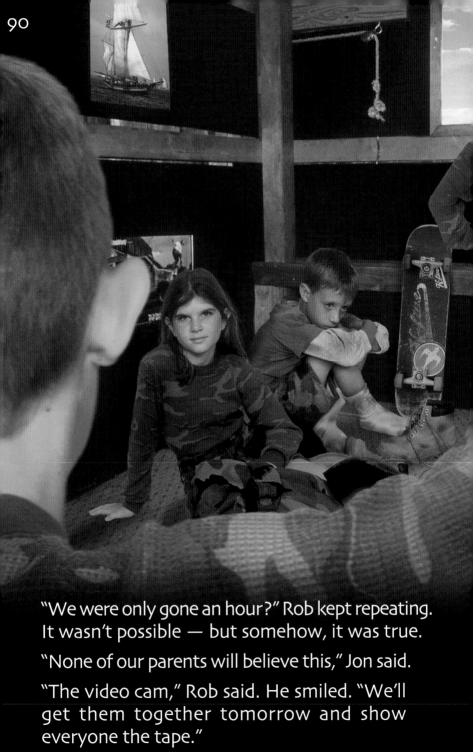

"We were only gone an hour?" Rob kept repeating. It wasn't possible — but somehow, it was true.

"None of our parents will believe this," Jon said.

"The video cam," Rob said. He smiled. "We'll get them together tomorrow and show everyone the tape."

"Good idea," Mariah said.

"And not a single word to any of them until then," said Jon.

"And we never tell any other kids," Mikey added. "It's our secret."

Everyone promised.

It was a perfect plan.

But later, in the
silence of the night...

94

What happens when T-Rex comes through the portal the next morning? Will the Time Soldiers be able to protect their own neighborhood? Don't miss their next fantastic adventure. For a sneak preview, join them at:

www.timesoldiers.com

Sunday 5:13 A.M. Guess who's coming for breakfast?

To be continued

The Time Soldiers® Series:

Don't miss the ultimate reading adventure!

"BRILLIANT!"

Barry Cunningham, original publisher of **HARRY POTTER** in the U.K.

"**REX** and The **TIME SOLDIERS** ® is a must read for every elementary school student. It's action-packed with incredible digitally enhanced photographs, making these dinosaurs the most lifelike ever seen. This is sure to become a favorite of every young boy in America."

Linda Wood Fiacco, Teacher/Reading Specialist (25 years)

"These books are different from anything I have ever seen.
My students wanted to skip recess to finish reading REX (book #1 in the series).
Kids everywhere are going to flip over them."

L. Rilbik, Reading Specialist/Teacher

"If the books are left lying open, a circle of children gathers around them...we have had informal (spontaneous) readings BY children FOR their friends... they all go through the pages together."

S. Peters, Children's Librarian

ISBN 978-1-4206-8940-2

50699

9 781420 689402